CROCHET
BOUTIQUE

◆ ◇◇◇◇◇◇◇◇◇◇◇◇◇◇◇◇ ◆ ◇◇◇◇◇◇◇◇◇◇◇◇◇◇◇◇ ◆

CROCHET BOUTIQUE

30 Simple, Stylish Hats, Bags & Accessories

rachael oglesby

◆ ◆ ◆

LARK CRAFTS
Asheville

Editor
Amanda Carestio

Tech Editor
Amy Polcyn

Art Director and Interior Designer
Megan Kirby

Art Assistant
Meagan Shirlen

Cover Designer
Pamela Norman

Illustrator
Orrin Lundgren

Photographer
Emily Ogden

LARK CRAFTS

An Imprint of Sterling Publishing
387 Park Avenue South
New York, NY 10016

If you have questions or comments about this
book, please visit: larkcrafts.com

Library of Congress Cataloging-in-Publication Data

Oglesby, Rachael.
 Crochet boutique : 30 simple, stylish hats, bags & accessories / Rachael Oglesby.
   p. cm.
 Includes bibliographical references and index.
 ISBN 978-1-60059-926-2 (alk. paper)
 1. Crocheting--Patterns. I. Title.
 TT825.O33 2012
 746.43'4--dc23

                              2011047737

10 9 8 7 6 5 4 3 2 1

First Edition

Published by Lark Crafts
An Imprint of Sterling Publishing Co., Inc.
387 Park Avenue South, New York, NY 10016

Text and Photography © 2012, Rachael Oglesby
Illustrations © 2012, Lark Crafts, an Imprint of Sterling Publishing Co., Inc., unless otherwise specified

Distributed in Canada by Sterling Publishing,
c/o Canadian Manda Group, 165 Dufferin Street
Toronto, Ontario, Canada M6K 3H6

Distributed in the United Kingdom by GMC Distribution Services,
Castle Place, 166 High Street, Lewes, East Sussex, England BN7 1XU

Distributed in Australia by Capricorn Link (Australia) Pty Ltd.,
P.O. Box 704, Windsor, NSW 2756 Australia

Manufactured in China

ISBN 13: 978-1-60059-926-2

For information about custom editions, special sales, and premium and corporate purchases, please
contact Sterling Special Sales Department at 800-805-5489 or specialsales@sterlingpub.com.

Requests for information about desk and examination copies available to college and university professors
must be submitted to academic@larkbooks.com. Our complete policy can be found at www.larkcrafts.com.

contents

introduction

Crochet has long-held a reputation (undeserved, I believe) for being bulky, stiff, tacky, too folksy (those '70s wonders I do cherish), and altogether unpolished. I'd like to challenge that notion.

My approach to crochet design is to make projects that are both on trend yet have a timeless quality to them. Each item I make is designed to fill a hole in my wardrobe or to serve as a statement piece to accent it—something that would seem at home in a street style photo of today, yet would remain a staple for many years to come. I hope you find my designs do just that.

This book explores the most fundamental crochet stitches and techniques in order to show you the variety of boutique-worthy projects you can create with only the basics under your belt. The projects are organized by type—hats, scarves and cowls, bags and accessories, and stitched items to cozy up your home—all scaled by difficulty levels: beginner, easy, and intermediate. Grab your hook and stitch up...

- **Stylish Items to Adorn Yourself:** Make a wagon wheel beret in every color!
- **Cherished Gifts to Make for Your Loved Ones:** Share the warmth with some cozy fingerless mittens.
- **Fashionable Accents for Your Home:** Sweeten your space with a heart garland.

Are you just getting started with crochet or in need of a quick refresher? There's a Basic Stitches & Techniques section at the back of the book (page 120); start there or use the section as a resource if you run into questions along the way.

I hope you enjoy the act of creating these projects as much as you do wearing them or giving them, and that crochet becomes a cherished accent to your life as it has my own.

—*Rachael*

getting started

So many elements go into the outcome of a finished crochet project—whether it be the stitches used, hook size, color choice, yarn weight, or different fibers—that you can create a wide range of beautiful and unique items by simply experimenting with basic stitches and varying combinations. The projects in this book explore these most fundamental crochet stitches and techniques in order to show you the variety of projects you can create with basic techniques, especially when paired with fun yarn. A large hook and thin yarn can create a beautiful lace-like effect. Bulky yarn in a dramatic color can create a quick-to-stitch statement piece. An alpaca yarn will yield results different from a soft cotton yarn of the same weight. You've got so many options ... for maximum boutique appeal!

Yarn

In creating the patterns for this book, I selected yarns that were easily accessible to the beginner, but still enticing to more seasoned crocheters. I factored in ease of availability and price, but most importantly, how well each yarn lent itself to the project at hand. Yarn weights and gauge are given in each project which make for quick and easy substitution should you choose to select a yarn more suited to your tastes and needs. Take a peek on page 126 for a helpful substitution chart.

Synthetics

The synthetic most commonly used in this book is acrylic. Acrylic yarns are an inexpensive option and are perfect for the beginner who may not want to invest in luxury yarn for their first project. Though they once held a bad reputation as tough and scratchy, synthetics today have since come a long way. There are now many different types of synthetic fibers that are both easy to maintain and feel soft and nice against the skin. Synthetics (along with natural fibers such as cotton and bamboo) are also a popular option among vegans since they contain no animal fiber.

Natural fibers

Natural fiber yarns are those made from plant or animal fibers. Examples of animal fiber yarns are wool, alpaca, cashmere, or mohair. Plant fiber yarns may be made from cotton, bamboo, linen, or hemp, among others. Each fiber is known for the different benefit it provides. For example, cotton is known to be durable and good for household items while wool is known for its warmth and moisture-wicking properties. Each fiber has its own unique set of properties, and you'll quickly find your favorites among them.

Blended yarns

Blended yarns are created with two or more different types of fibers to create a completely new and, at times, more durable yarn that contains the best properties of each. Blended yarns may mix synthetics with animal fibers, animal fibers with plant fibers, or any combination of the three. These yarns are often a nice stepping-stone from synthetics to luxury yarns since they allow you to experiment with new fibers while being a bit more budget friendly than their 100% natural counterparts.

Hooks & Tools

One of the benefits of crochet is that it does not require many materials to begin. The basic essentials are a hook, yarn, scissors, and a yarn needle to fasten off.

Hooks

Crochet hooks come in many different sizes, materials, textures, and even colors. Hooks may be made from steel, plastic, aluminum, or bamboo. The choice of material is often a matter of personal preference and aesthetic. There are also many ergonomic hooks now available as well as hooks with rubber grips which allow them to sit more easily in your hand, causing less stress on your joints.

Hooks also range in size. The smallest of hooks are most often used with thread for lacemaking and doilies while the largest hooks are often paired with the thicker, chunky yarns for items that work up more quickly. Hooks are typically labeled with their size—a number, letter, or both. See the hook size chart on page 126 for more information on hook sizing.

Scissors

It is always best to keep a pair of scissors nearby while crocheting for snipping ends or joining colors. Most any type of scissors will do as long as they are sharp enough to snip through your yarn, though you may find a small pair easiest to carry along with your projects.

Yarn needle

A yarn needle is similar to an embroidery needle except that the tip is blunt and the eye is large enough for a variety of yarn sizes to pass through. It is helpful for finishing your projects and weaving those loose ends into your item as the final step.

Tape measure

A tape measure is always nice to have on hand, particularly to measure gauge when starting your project and for any needed measurements while finishing and joining seams.

Gauge

Gauge is the number of rows and stitches found in a specified area. In this book, gauge is most often determined by the number of rows and stitches it takes to create a 4"/10cm square. You'll find this info at the beginning of each pattern. Checking your gauge is useful since each person stitches differently; some may lean towards looser tension while others may stitch more tightly. Such differences may result in finished items that are not the size you intended, especially if you don't check the gauge first. Gauge is most important for items that are fitted. It is not quite as important for items such as scarves where a precise fit is not required; however, it is still recommended.

To make a gauge swatch, start with the recommended yarn and hook size. Crochet a square that is at least 4"/10cm wide by 4"/10cm tall (you may choose to make your square slightly larger if you like, in which case you'd measure an interior swatch that measures 4"/10cm square). Once your square is stitched, lay the swatch flat. Using a tape measure to mark off 4"/10cm, count the number of stitches across and then the number of rows down to see if they match the given gauge.

If the gauge is off, this is often easily fixed by changing hook size. If you find that there are more stitches and rows than the gauge given, your stitches are too small; try the next largest hook. If the opposite is true, try moving down to a smaller hook size.

skill levels

You'll find a range of project skill levels in this book. Here's a little information on what those levels mean. If you're new to crochet, start with a beginner project and move up as you build confidence.

Beginner

This level uses the most basic crochet stitches. Most projects at this level are worked in one piece and do not require any further construction or seaming.

Easy

Projects in this level typically use simple pattern stitches or may use a variety of basic stitches. They require a bit more attention and focus than beginner projects.

Intermediate

Projects in the intermediate range use more intricate pattern stitches and more advanced techniques. They may require some construction and seaming and may include other techniques such as sewing or embroidery.

THE
PROJECTS

Openwork Beanie

With its open chain design and single crochet band,
you'd never guess this hat is made from just two
stitches. A perfect beanie for the new crocheter.

◆ ◆ ◆

finished measurements

◆ 8½" tall x 18" circumference (22cm x 46cm)

materials and tools

◆ Lion Brand Wool-Ease Chunky (80% acrylic, 20% wool; 5oz/140g = 153yd/140m): 1 skein, color spice #135—approx 153yd/140m of bulky weight yarn ⑤

◆ Crochet hook: 9.00mm (size N-13 U.S.) or size to obtain gauge

◆ Yarn needle

gauge

◆ 9 sc and 10 rows = 4"/10cm

Always take time to check your gauge.

stitches used

◆ chain (ch)

◆ slip stitch (sl st)

◆ single crochet (sc)

Openwork Beanie

instructions

Ch 4, join with a sl st in first ch to form a ring.

Rnd 1: Ch 1 (counts as first sc here and throughout), work 15 sc into ring, join with sl st in top of beg ch—16 sc.

Rnd 2: *Ch 3, skip next st, sc in next st; rep from * around ending with ch-3, join with sl st in beg ch-3.

Rnd 3: Work sl st in next ch, *ch 4, sc in next sp; rep from * around, ending with ch-4, join with sl st in beg ch-4.

Rnd 4: Work sl st in next 2 ch, *ch 5, sc in next sp; rep from * around, ending with ch-5, join with sl st in beg ch-5.

Rnd 5: Rep rnd 4.

Rnd 6: Work sl st in next 2 ch, *ch 6, sc in next sp; rep from * around, ending with ch-6, join with sl st in beg ch-6.

Rnd 7: Work sl st in next 3 ch, *ch 6, sc in next sp; rep from * around, ending with ch-6, join with sl st in beg ch-6.

Rnds 8–10: Rep rnd 7.

Rnd 11: Ch 1, work 5 sc in each sp around, join with sl st to beg ch-1—40 sc.

Rnds 12–16: Ch 1, sc in each st around, join with sl st in beg ch-1.

Fasten off.

Finishing

Using yarn needle, weave in ends.

Slouchy Beanie

◆ ⬦⬦⬦⬦⬦⬦⬦⬦⬦⬦⬦⬦⬦⬦⬦⬦⬦⬦ ◆ ⬦⬦⬦⬦⬦⬦⬦⬦⬦⬦⬦⬦⬦⬦⬦⬦⬦ ◆

The classic beanie gets a fashion-forward update. The result—a look that's perfect for days in the city or wherever you roam.

◆ ◆ ◆

finished measurements

- 11" tall by 18½" circumference (stretches to fit) (28cm x 47cm)

materials and tools

- Lion Brand Wool-Ease Worsted Weight (80% acrylic, 20% wool; 3oz/85g = 197yd/180m): 1 skein, color blue heather #107—approx 197yd/180m of worsted weight yarn (4)
- Crochet hook: 5.50mm (size I-9 U.S.) or size to obtain gauge
- Yarn needle

gauge

- 15 dc and 8 rows = 4"/10cm

Always take time to check your gauge.

stitches used

- chain (ch)
- slip stitch (sl st)
- double crochet (dc)
- single crochet (sc)

Note: Optional color shown on cover is cranberry #138.

Slouchy Beanie

instructions

Ch 3, join with a sl st in first ch to form a ring.

Rnd 1: Ch 2 (counts as first dc here and throughout), work 9 dc in ring, join with sl st in top of beg ch-2—10 dc.

Rnd 2: Ch 2, dc in same st as beg ch-2, work 2 dc in each st around, join with sl st in top of beg ch-2—20 dc.

Rnd 3: Ch 2, 2 dc in next st, *dc, 2 dc in next st; rep from * around, join with sl st in top of beg ch-2—30 dc.

Rnd 4: Ch 2, dc, 2 dc in next st, *dc in next 2 sts, 2 dc in next st; rep from * around, join with sl st in top of beg ch-2—40 dc.

Rnd 5: Ch 2, dc in next 2 sts, 2 dc in next st, *dc in next 3 sts, 2 dc in next st; rep from * around, join with sl st in top of beg ch-2—50 dc.

Rnd 6: Ch 2, dc in next 8 sts, 2 dc in next st, *dc in next 9 sts, 2 dc in next st; rep from * around, join with sl st in top of beg ch-2—55 dc.

Rnd 7: Ch 2, dc in next 9 sts, 2 dc in next st, *dc in next 10 sts, 2 dc in next st; rep from * around, join with sl st in top of beg ch-2—60 dc.

Rnd 8: Ch 2, dc in next 10 sts, 2 dc in next st, *dc in next 11 sts, 2 dc in next st; rep from * around, join with sl st in top of beg ch-2—65 dc.

Rnd 9: Ch 2, dc in next 11 sts, 2 dc in next st, *dc in next 12 sts, 2 dc in next st; rep from * around, join with sl st in top of beg ch-2—70 dc.

Rnd 10: Ch 2, dc in each st around, join with sl st in top of beg ch-2—70 dc.

Rnds 11–18: Rep rnd 10.

Rnd 19: Ch 1, sc in each st around, join with sl st in beg ch-1.

Rnds 20–28: Rep rnd 19.

Fasten off.

Finishing

Using yarn needle,
weave in ends.

Pompom (optional)

Cut a 10"/25cm strand of
yarn and set aside. Holding
end of yarn and feeding from
skein in left hand between
thumb and index finger,
wrap around four fingers of
hand 115 times. Cut yarn.

Take 10"/25cm strand of yarn
and tie around middle of yarn
on hand. Pull knot tightly as you
pull yarn off fingers. Double
knot to secure. Insert scissors in loops and cut open.
Trim pompom to desired size,
leaving ends of long strand
for attaching to beanie. Tie
pompom to top of beanie with a
double knot and weave in ends.

Boy Beanie

Guys love hats that work: A chunky wool-blend
yarn will keep his ears warm.

finished measurements

◆ 8" tall x 18" circumference (stretches to fit) (20cm x 46cm)

materials and tools

◆ Lion Brand Wool-Ease Thick and Quick (80% wool, 20% acrylic; 6oz/170g = 108yd/98m): (A), 1 skein, color oatmeal #123; (B), 1 skein, color barley #124—approx 216yd/196m of super bulky weight yarn (6)

◆ Crochet hook: 11.50mm (size P-15 U.S.) or size to obtain gauge

◆ Yarn needle

gauge

◆ 7 dc and 4 rows = 4"/10cm

Always take time to check your gauge.

stitches used

◆ chain (ch)

◆ slip stitch (sl st)

◆ double crochet (dc)

◆ single crochet (sc)

◆ double crochet two stitches together (dc2tog)

Boy Beanie

instructions

With A, ch 3, join with a sl st in first ch to form a ring.

Rnd 1: Ch 2 (counts as first dc here and throughout), work 14 dc in ring, join with sl st in top of beg ch—15 dc.

Rnd 2: Ch 2, dc in same st as beg ch-2, work 2 dc in each st around, join with sl st in top of beg ch-2—30 dc.

Rnds 3–4: Ch 2, dc in each st around, join with sl st in top of beg ch-2—30 dc. Join B.

Rnds 5–7: Ch 2, dc in each st around, join with sl st in top of beg ch-2—30 dc. Join A.

Rnds 8–9: Ch 1, sc in each st around, join with sl st in beg ch-1.

Fasten off.

Finishing

Using yarn needle, weave in ends.

Sunburst Beret

◆ ⬦⬦⬦⬦⬦⬦⬦⬦⬦⬦⬦⬦⬦⬦ ◆ ⬦⬦⬦⬦⬦⬦⬦⬦⬦⬦⬦⬦⬦⬦ ◆

Inspired by the traditional wagon wheel design,
this wool-blend beret stitches up quickly
but looks like it took days.

◆ ◆ ◆

skill level ◆ beginner

finished measurements

- Diameter 11"/28 cm

materials and tools

- Caron Country (75% microdenier acrylic, 25% merino wool; 3oz/85g = 185yd/170m): 1 skein, color deep purple #0014—approx 185yd/170m of worsted weight yarn (4)
- Crochet hook: 5.50mm (size I-9 U.S.) or size to obtain gauge
- Yarn needle

gauge

- 12 dc and 7 rows = 4"/10cm

Always take time to check your gauge.

stitches used

- chain (ch)
- slip stitch (sl st)
- double crochet (dc)
- single crochet (sc)

Note: Optional colors shown are spruce #0013 and gilded age #0011.

Sunburst Beret

instructions

Ch 3, join with a sl st in first ch to form a ring.

Rnd 1: Ch 3 (counts as first dc), work 19 dc into ring, join with sl st in top of beg ch-3—20 dc.

Rnd 2: Ch 4 (counts as first dc, ch 1), *dc in next dc, ch 1; rep from * around, join with sl st in 3rd ch of beg ch-4—20 dc.

Rnd 3: Ch 5 (counts as first dc, ch 2), *dc in next dc, ch 2; rep from * around, join with sl st in 3rd ch of beg ch-5—20 dc.

Rnd 4: Sl st to first ch-2 sp, ch 3, dc in same sp, ch 2, *2 dc in next ch-2 sp, ch 2; rep from * around, join with sl st in top of beg ch-3—20 2-dc clusters.

Rnd 5: Sl st to first ch-2 sp, ch 3, 2 dc in same sp, ch 2, *3 dc in next ch-2 sp, ch 2; rep from * around, join with sl st in top of beg ch-3—20 3-dc clusters.

Rnds 6–9: Sl st to first ch-2 sp, ch 3, 3 dc in same sp, ch 2, *4 dc in next ch-2 sp, ch 2; rep from * around, join with sl st in top of beg ch-3—20 4-dc clusters.

Rnd 10: Sl st to first ch-2 sp, ch 3, 2 dc in same sp, ch 2, *3 dc in next sp, ch 2; rep from * around, join with sl st in top of beg ch-3—20 3-dc clusters.

Rnd 11: Sl st to first ch-2 sp, ch 3, dc in same sp, ch 2, *2 dc in next sp, ch 2; rep from * around, join with sl st in top of beg ch-3—20 2-dc clusters.

Rnd 12: Sl st to first ch-2 sp, ch 3, dc in same sp, ch 1, *2 dc in next sp, ch 1; rep from * around, join with sl st in top of beg ch-3—20 2-dc clusters.

Rnd 13: Ch 1, sc in each dc and ch-1 sp around, join with sl st in beg ch-1—60 sts.

Rnd 14: Ch 1, sc in each sc around, join with sl st in beg ch-1—60 sts.

Fasten off.

Finishing

Using yarn needle, weave in ends.

Floppy Sun Hat

◆ ⬦⬦⬦⬦⬦⬦⬦⬦⬦⬦⬦⬦⬦⬦⬦⬦⬦⬦ ◆ ⬦⬦⬦⬦⬦⬦⬦⬦⬦⬦⬦⬦⬦⬦⬦⬦⬦⬦ ◆

*Wear the brim any way you choose
(it's adorable flipped up). The lightweight,
breathable yarn feels fine year-round.*

◆ ◆ ◆

skill level ◆ easy

finished measurements

- 10½" tall x 20" circumference (27cm x 51cm)

materials and tools

- Lion Brand Cotton-Ease (50% cotton, 50% acrylic; 3.5oz/100g = 207yd/188m): 2 skeins, color taupe #122—approx 414yd/376m of worsted weight yarn (4)

- Crochet hook: 9.00mm (size N-13 U.S.) or size to obtain gauge

- Yarn needle

gauge

- 10 sc and 11 rows = 4"/10cm

Always take time to check your gauge.

stitches used

- chain (ch)
- slip stitch (sl st)
- double crochet (dc)
- single crochet (sc)

Floppy Sun Hat

instructions

Ch 3, join with a sl st in first ch to form a ring.

Rnd 1: Ch 1 (counts as first sc here and throughout), work 14 sc into ring, join with sl st in top of beg ch-1—15 sc.

Rnd 2: Ch 1, sc in same st as beg ch-1, work 2 sc in each st around, join with sl st in top of beg ch-1—30 sc.

Rnd 3: Ch 1, sc, work 2 sc in next st, *sc in next 2 sts, 2 sc in next st; rep from * around, join with sl st in top of beg ch-1—40 sc.

Rnd 4: Ch 1, sk 1, work 4 dc in next st (shell made), sk 1, *sc, sk 1, work 4 dc in next st, sk 1; rep from * around, join with sl st in beg ch-1—10 shells.

Rnd 5: Ch 2 (counts as first dc), work dc in same st, sk 2 sts, sc in next st, sk 1, *work 4 dc in next st, sk 2, sc in next st, sk 1; rep from * around. Work 2 dc in same st as beg ch-2, join to top of beg ch-2—10 shells.

Rnd 6: Ch 1, sk 1, work 4 dc in next st, sk 2, *sc in next st, sk 1, work 4 dc in next st, sk 2; rep from * around, join with sl st in beg ch-1—10 shells.

Rnds 7–10: Rep rnds 5 and 6.

Rnd 11: Ch 1, sc in each st around, join with sl st in beg ch-1—50 sc.

Rnd 12: Ch 1, sc in next 8 sts, 2 sc in next st, *sc in next 9 sts, 2 sc in next st; rep from * around, join with sl st in beg ch-1—55 sc.

Rnd 13: Ch 1, sc in next 9 sts, 2 sc in next st, *sc in next 10 sts, 2 sc in next st; rep from * around, join with sl st in beg ch-1—60 sc.

Rnd 14: Ch 1, sc in each st around, join with sl st in beg ch-1—60 sc.

Rnd 15: Ch 1, sc in next 10 sts, 2 sc in next st, *sc in next 11 sts, 2 sc in next st; rep from * around, join with sl st in beg ch-1—65 sc.

Rnd 16: Ch 1, sc in each st around, join with sl st in beg ch-1—65 sc.

Rnd 17: Ch 1, sc in next 11 sts, 2 sc in next st, *sc in next 12 sts, 2 sc in next st; rep from * around, join with sl st in beg ch-1—70 sc.

Rnd 18: Ch 1, sc in each st around, join with sl st in beg ch-1—70 sc.

Rnd 19: Ch 1, sc in next 12 sts, 2 sc in next st, *sc in next 13 sts, 2 sc in next st; rep from * around, join with sl st in beg ch-1—75 sc.

Rnd 20: Ch 1, sc in each st around, join with sl st to beg ch-1—75 sc.

Fasten off.

Finishing

Using yarn needle, weave in ends.

Adjustable Bow

Thread two long strands of yarn through yarn needle and weave through first rnd of sc at top of brim. Pull through and leave ends long enough to tie bow to desired length. Trim ends as needed.

Bubble Beret

◆ ✕✕✕✕✕✕✕✕✕✕✕✕✕✕ ◆ ✕✕✕✕✕✕✕✕✕✕✕✕✕✕ ◆

The soft touch of baby alpaca yarn plays well
with the stitched bobble texture.

◆ ◆ ◆

finished measurements

- Diameter 10½"/27cm

materials and tools

- Plymouth Yarn Baby Alpaca Brush (80% baby alpaca, 20% acrylic; 1.75 oz/50g = 110yd/101m): 2 skeins, color blush #2671—approx 220yd/202m of bulky weight yarn 5
- Crochet hook: 5.00mm (size H-8 U.S.) or size to obtain gauge
- Yarn needle

gauge

- 13 dc and 7 rows = 4"/10cm

Always take time to check your gauge.

stitches used

- chain (ch)
- slip stitch (sl st)
- double crochet (dc)
- single crochet (sc)
- bobble (bo)
- double crochet two stitches together (dc2tog)

pattern stitch

- Bobble: [Yo, insert hook into st, yo and draw up a loop, yo, draw through 2 loops] 5 times in same st, yo and draw through all 6 loops on hook.

◆ Bubble Beret

instructions

Ch 3, join with a sl st in first ch to form a ring.

Rnd 1: Ch 2 (counts as first dc, here and throughout), work 17 dc in ring, join with sl st in top of beg ch-2—18 sts.

Rnd 2: Ch 2, work 1 dc in same st as beg ch, work 2 dc in each dc, join with sl st in top of beg ch-2—36 sts.

Rnd 3: Ch 1, sc, *work bo in next st, sc in next 2 sts; rep from * around to last 2 sts. Work bo in next st, sc in last st, join with sl st in beg ch-1—12 bobbles.

Rnd 4: Ch 2, dc, work 2 dc in next st, *dc in next 2 sts, 2 dc in next st; rep from * around, join with sl st in top of beg ch-2—248 sts.

Rnd 5: Ch 2, dc in next 2 sts, work 2 dc in next st, *dc in next 3 sts, 2 dc in next st; rep from * around, join with sl st in top of beg ch-2—60 sts.

Rnd 6: Rep rnd 3—20 bobbles.

Rnd 7: Ch 2, dc in next 3 sts, work 2 dc in next st, *dc in next 4 sts, 2 dc in next st; rep from * around, join with sl st in top of beg ch-2—72 sts.

Rnd 8: Ch 2, dc in next 4 sts, work 2 dc in next st, *dc in next 5 sts, 2 dc in next st; rep from * around, join with sl st in top of beg ch-2—84 sts.

Rnd 9: Rep rnd 3—28 bobbles.

Rnd 10: Ch 2, dc in next 5 sts, work 2 dc in next st, *dc in next 6 sts, 2 dc in next st; rep from * around, join with sl st in top of beg ch-2—96 sts.

Rnd 11: Ch 2, dc in next 5 sts, dc2tog (counts as 1 st here and throughout), *dc in next 6 dc, dc2tog; rep from * around, join with sl st in top of beg ch-2—84 sts.

Rnd 12: Rep rnd 3—28 bobbles total.

Rnd 13: Ch 2, dc in next 4 sts, dc2tog, *dc in next 5 dc, dc2tog; rep from * around, join with sl st in top of beg ch-2—72 sts.

Rnd 14: Ch 2, dc in next 3 sts, dc2tog, *dc in next 4 dc, dc2tog; rep from * around, join with sl st in top of beg ch-2—60 sts.

Rnd 15: Rep rnd 3—20 bobbles.

Rnd 16: Ch 2, dc in each st, join with sl st in top of beg ch-2—60 sts.

Rnds 17–18: Ch 1, sc in each st, join with sl st in top of beg ch-1.

Fasten off.

Finishing

Using yarn needle, weave in ends.

Bonnie Beret

◆ ✕✕✕✕✕✕✕✕✕✕✕✕✕✕ ◆ ✕✕✕✕✕✕✕✕✕✕✕✕✕✕ ◆

This simple beret nods to Faye Dunaway's classic look in Bonnie and Clyde— updated here in a chunky yarn.

◆ ◆ ◆

finished measurements

◆ Diameter 11"/28cm

materials and tools

◆ Lion Brand Wool-Ease Thick and Quick (80% wool, 20% acrylic; 6oz/170g = 108yd/98m): 1 skein, color butterscotch #189—approx 108yd/98m of super bulky weight yarn (6)

◆ Crochet hook: 11.50mm (size P-15 U.S.) or size to obtain gauge

◆ Yarn needle

gauge

◆ 7 dc and 4 rows = 4"/10cm

Always take time to check your gauge.

stitches used

◆ chain (ch)

◆ slip stitch (sl st)

◆ double crochet (dc)

◆ single crochet (sc)

◆ double crochet two stitches together (dc2tog)

Note: Optional color shown is lemongrass #132.

Bonnie Beret

instructions

Ch 3, join with a sl st in first ch to form a ring.

Rnd 1: Ch 2, (counts as first dc here and throughout), work 14 dc into ring, join with sl st in top of beg ch-2—15 dc.

Rnd 2: Ch 2, dc in same st as beg ch, work 2 dc in each st around, join with sl st in top of beg ch-2—30 dc.

Rnd 3: Ch 2, dc, work 2 dc in next st, *dc in next 2 sts, 2 dc in next st; rep from * around, join with sl st in top of beg ch-2—40 dc.

Rnds 4–5: Ch 2, dc in each st around, join with sl st in top of beg ch-2—40 dc.

Rnd 6: Ch 2, dc, dc2tog (counts as 1 dc), *dc in next 2 sts, dc2tog; rep from * around, join with sl st in top of beg ch-2—30 dc.

Rnd 7: Ch 2, dc in each st around, join with sl st to top of beg ch-2—30 dc.

Rnds 8–9: Ch 1, sc in each st around, join with sl st to beg ch-1.

Fasten off.

Finishing

Using yarn needle, weave in ends.

Chunky Ribbed Scarf

◆ ◇◇◇◇◇◇◇◇◇◇◇◇◇◇ ◆ ◇◇◇◇◇◇◇◇◇◇◇◇◇ ◆

Stitched in super soft chunky yarn and long enough to wrap around you twice, this classic ribbed scarf will be your new favorite.

◆ ◆ ◆

skill level ◇ beginner

finished measurements

• 8" wide x 96" long (20cm x 244cm)

materials and tools

• Plymouth Yarn Baby Alpaca Grande (100% baby alpaca, 3.5oz/100g=110yd/101m): 3 skeins, color wheat #202—approx 330yd/303m of bulky weight yarn ❺

• Crochet hook: 15.75mm (size Q-19 U.S.) or size to obtain gauge

• Yarn needle

gauge

• 5 sc and 8 rows = 4"/10cm

Always take time to check your gauge.

stitches used

• chain (ch)

• single crochet (sc)

Chunky Ribbed Scarf

instructions

Ch 116.

Row 1: Ch 1, sc in each ch across—115 sts.

Row 2: Ch 1, turn, sc in back loop of each st.

Rows 3–16: Rep row 2.

Fasten off.

Finishing

Using yarn needle, weave in ends.

Cuddle Cowl

◆ ⬥⬥⬥⬥⬥⬥⬥⬥⬥⬥⬥⬥⬥⬥⬥ ◆ ⬥⬥⬥⬥⬥⬥⬥⬥⬥⬥⬥⬥⬥⬥⬥ ◆

*Ribbed on one side and smooth on the other,
sport this cowl either way you like or
switch it up as the mood strikes.*

◆ ◆ ◆

skill level ◈ beginner

finished measurements

- 18" deep x 28" circumference (46cm x 71cm)

materials and tools

- Lion Brand Hometown USA (100% acrylic; 5oz/142g = 108yd/98m): 2 skeins, color Dallas grey #149—approx 216yd/196m of super bulky weight yarn (6)
- Crochet hook: 15.75mm (size Q-19 U.S.) or size to obtain gauge
- Yarn needle

gauge

- 5 sc and 5 rows = 4"/10cm

Always take time to check your gauge.

stitches used

- chain (ch)
- slip stitch (sl st)
- single crochet (sc)

Cuddle Cowl

instructions

Ch 36, join with a sl st in first ch to form a ring.

Rnd 1: Ch 1 (counts as first sc here and throughout), sc in back loop only in each st around, join with sl st in beg ch-1—36 sts.

Rnds 2–24: Rep rnd 1.

Fasten off.

Finishing

Using yarn needle, weave in ends.

Infinity Circle Scarf

Extra lux baby alpaca yarn stitches up to make a scarf that's soft as a cloud yet warmer than your favorite blanket. Wear it long or doubled up.

skill level ◆ easy

finished measurements

♦ 10" wide x 50" circumference (25cm x 127cm)

materials and tools

♦ Plymouth Yarn Baby Alpaca Ampato Aran Weight (100% baby alpaca; 3.5oz/100g = 128yd/117m): 3 hanks, color #901—approx 384yd/351m of aran weight yarn ❹

♦ Crochet hook: 6.50mm (size K-10.5 U.S.) or size to obtain gauge

♦ Yarn needle

gauge

♦ 10 dc and 6 rows = 4"/10cm

Always take time to check your gauge.

stitches used

♦ chain (ch)

♦ slip stitch (sl st)

♦ double crochet (dc)

♦ single crochet (sc)

♦ cluster (cl)

pattern stitch

♦ Cluster (cl): [Yo, insert hook in next st, yo, draw up a loop, yo, draw through 2 loops] 3 times in same st, yo and draw through all 4 loops on hook.

Infinity Circle Scarf

instructions

Ch 120, join with a sl st in first ch to form a ring.

Rnd 1: Ch 2, [yo, insert hook in same sp, yo, draw up a loop, yo, draw through 2 loops] 2 times, yo and draw through all 3 loops on hook, ch 1, sk 1 ch, *work cl in next st, ch 1, sk 1; rep from * around, join with sl st in top of first cluster—60 clusters.

Rnd 2: Work sl st in first ch-1 sp, ch 2, [yo, insert hook in same sp, yo, draw up a loop, yo, draw through 2 loops] 2 times, yo and draw through all 3 loops on hook, ch 1, *in next ch-1 sp work cl, ch 1; rep from * around, join with sl st at top of first cluster—60 clusters.

Rnds 3–10: Rep rnd 2.

Rnd 11: Ch 1, sc in next ch-1 sp, *sc in top of next cl, sc in next ch-1 sp; rep from * around, join with sl st in beg ch-1—120 sc.

Rnds 12–13: Ch 1, sc in each st around, join with sl st in beg ch-1.

Fasten off.

Finishing

Join yarn in any ch-1 sp of rnd 1, ch 1, sc in next cl, *sc in next ch-1 sp, sc in next cl; rep from * around, join with sl st in beg ch-1—120 sc. Work in sc for 2 rnds more.

Fasten off. Using yarn needle, weave in ends.

Lace Shell Wrap

◆ ◇◇◇◇◇◇◇◇◇◇◇◇◇◇◇◇◇◇◇ ◆ ◇◇◇◇◇◇◇◇◇◇◇◇◇◇◇◇◇◇◇ ◆

*Dress up spaghetti straps with this delicate
lace wrap, just the thing for those
cooler summer evenings.*

◆ ◆ ◆

skill level ◆ easy

finished measurements

• 18" wide x 74" long (46cm x 188cm)

materials and tools

• Caron Spa (75% microdenier acrylic, 25% rayon from bamboo; 3oz/85g = 251yd/230m): 3 skeins, color clay pot #0015—approx 753yd/690m of DK weight yarn **③**

• Crochet hook: 9.00mm (size N-13 U.S.) or size to obtain gauge

• Yarn needle

• 9½"/24cm cardboard square

gauge

• 10 dc and 5 rows = 4"/10cm

Always take time to check your gauge.

stitches used

• chain (ch)

• double crochet (dc)

Lace Shell Wrap

instructions

When making slip knot, leave tail 9½"/24cm long to blend with fringe.

Ch 85.

Row 1: (4 dc, ch 2, 2 dc) in 8th ch from hook (7 skipped ch count as first dc and 4 skipped ch), *skip next 8 ch, (4 dc, ch 2, 2 dc) in next ch (shell made); rep from * across to last 5 ch, skip next 4 ch, dc in last ch—9 shells.

Row 2: Ch 3 (counts as first dc here and throughout), turn, *(4 dc, ch 2, 2 dc) in each ch-2 sp across to last 5 dc, skip 4 dc, dc in last dc.

Rows 3–66: Rep row 2.

Fasten off, leaving tail 9½"/24cm long (blend with fringe).

Finishing

Fringe

Wrap yarn around 9½"/24cm cardboard square 90 times. Insert scissors under loops at one end and cut. Taking 4 strands at a time, attach fringe to ends of wrap as follows: Insert hook in st. Fold strands in half and place on hook, pull through st to form a loop. Draw ends through loop and pull tight to secure. At lower edge, attach fringe in each corner and in center of each skipped ch-8 sp. At top edge, attach fringe in each corner and between each shell.

Using yarn needle, weave in ends.

Chain Scarf

◆ ◇◇◇◇◇◇◇◇◇◇◇◇◇◇◇◇ ◆ ◇◇◇◇◇◇◇◇◇◇◇◇◇◇◇◇ ◆

Grab your hook and yarn, and get ready to count those chains. This scarf is 100% beginner friendly, but the results are totally chic.

◆ ◆ ◆

skill level ◆ beginner

finished measurements

- 14½" long/37cm

materials and tools

- Knit Picks Shine Worsted (60% pima cotton, 40% modal; 1.75oz/50g = 75yd/69m): 2 skeins, color currant #25362—approx 150yd/138m of worsted weight yarn (4)
- Crochet hook: 5.50mm (size I-9 U.S.) or size to obtain gauge
- Yarn needle

gauge

- 16 sc and 12 rows = 4"/10cm

Always take time to check your gauge.

stitches used

- chain (ch)
- slip stitch (sl st)
- single crochet (sc)

Chain Scarf

instructions

Square Base

Ch 11.

Row 1: Ch 1, sc in 2nd ch from hook and in each ch across, turn—10 sc.

Row 2: Ch 1, sc in each sc across.

Rows 3–10: Rep row 2.

Note: Each chain is joined on the opposite end from where it began, working back and forth, alternating sides across.

Chains

Chain 1: Ch 125, join with sl st in sc on bottom of square.

Chain 2: Ch 125, join with sl st in first sc at top of square.

Chain 3: Ch 125, join with sl st in same sc as the first chain on bottom of square—3 chains joined in the same st on each side.

Sl st in next st. Cont as established, working 3 ch in each st across—30 chains. Fasten off.

Finishing

Using yarn needle, weave in ends.

skill level ◆ easy

Textured Waves Scarf

◆ ⬦⬦⬦⬦⬦⬦⬦⬦⬦⬦⬦⬦⬦⬦⬦⬦ ◆ ⬦⬦⬦⬦⬦⬦⬦⬦⬦⬦⬦⬦⬦⬦⬦⬦ ◆

*A clever pattern of tall and short stitches creates
a wear-with-anything wave texture, lovely with
the lightly brushed appearance of this yarn.*

◆ ◆ ◆

finished measurements

◆ 7" wide x 88" long (18cm x 224cm)

materials and tools

◆ Caron Dazzleaire (80% acrylic, 20% nylon; 3oz/85g = 155yd/141m): 2 skeins, color pinot noir #0008—approx 310yd/282cm of bulky weight yarn (5)

◆ Crochet hook: 11.50mm (size P-15 U.S.) or size to obtain gauge

◆ Yarn needle

gauge

◆ 8 dc and 4 rows = 4"/10cm

Always take time to check your gauge.

stitches used

◆ chain (ch)

◆ treble crochet (tr)

◆ single crochet (sc)

Textured Waves Scarf

instructions

Ch 15.

Row 1: Sc in 2nd ch from hook (skipped ch counts as first sc), sc in next 3 ch, tr in next 5 ch, sc in next 5 ch—15 sts.

Note: Work in back loops only from here to end.

Rows 2 and 3: Ch 3 (counts as first tr), turn, tr in next 4 sts, sc in next 5 sts, tr in next 5 sts.

Rows 4 and 5: Ch 1 (counts as first sc), turn, sc in next 4 sts, tr in next 5 sts, sc in next 5 sts.

Rows 6–73: Rep rows 2–5.

Row 74: Rep row 2.

Fasten off.

Finishing

Using yarn needle, weave in ends.

Button Capelet

◆ ◇◇◇◇◇◇◇◇◇◇◇◇◇◇◇◇ ◆ ◇◇◇◇◇◇◇◇◇◇◇◇◇◇◇◇ ◆

*Inspired by the classic crochet ponchos from
the 70's, this capelet gets an update with bulky
yarn and large wooden buttons.*

◆ ◆ ◆

finished measurements

◆ 26" long x 49" lower circumference (buttoned) (66cm x 124cm)

materials and tools

◆ Lion Brand Wool-Ease Thick and Quick (80% wool, 20% acrylic; 6oz/170g = 108yd/98m): 3 skeins, color lemongrass #132—approx 324yd/294m of super bulky weight yarn ⑥

◆ Crochet hook: 15.75mm (size Q-19 U.S.) or size to obtain gauge

◆ Yarn needle

◆ Four 1½"/4cm wooden buttons

gauge

◆ 5 sc and 5 rows = 4"/10cm

Always take time to check your gauge.

stitches used

◆ chain (ch)

◆ slip stitch (sl st)

◆ single crochet (sc)

◆ double crochet (dc)

Button Capelet

instructions

Ch 34.

Row 1: Work dc in 4th ch from hook (first 3 ch count as first dc), dc in next 5 ch, work 2 dc in next ch, *work dc in next 7 ch, 2 dc in next ch; rep from * across—36 dc.

Row 2: Ch 2 (counts as first dc), turn. Sc in next st, *dc in next st, sc in next st; rep from * across.

Row 3: Rep row 2.

Row 4: Ch 2, turn. Dc in next 7 sts, work 2 dc in next st, *dc in next 8 sts, work 2 dc in next st; rep from * across—40 dc.

Rows 5–6: Rep row 2.

Row 7: Ch 2, turn. Dc in next 8 sts, work 2 dc in next st, *dc in next 9 sts, work 2 dc in next st; rep from * across to end—44 dc.

Rows 8–9: Rep row 2.

Row 10: Ch 2, turn. Dc in next 9 sts, work 2 dc in next st, *dc in next 10 sts, work 2 dc in next st; rep from * across—48 dc.

Rows 11–12: Rep row 2.

Row 13: Ch 2, turn. Dc in next 10 sts, work 2 dc in next st, *dc in next 11 sts, work 2 dc in next st; rep from * across—52 dc.

Rows 14–15: Rep row 2.

Row 16: Ch 2, turn. Dc in next 11 sts, work 2 dc in next st, *dc in next 12 sts, work 2 dc in next st; rep from * across—56 dc.

Rows 17–18: Ch 1, sc in each st across.

Fasten off.

Finishing

Join yarn at top edge, work 3 rows sc at neck. Do not fasten off.

Button Band

Row 1: Working down side edge, work 1 sc in each of the first 3 rows, then 2 sc in each of the next 16 rows, then 1 sc in each of the last 2 rows.

Row 2: Ch 1, turn. Work in sc in each sc across.

Row 3: Rep row 2. Fasten off.

Buttonhole Band

Row 1: On opposite side edge, work as for button band.

Row 2 (buttonhole row): Ch 1, turn. Work 1 sc in next st, ch 2, sk next 2 sts, *sc in next 5 sts, ch 2, sk next 2 sts; rep from * for a total of 4 buttonholes, sc to end. Fasten off.

Row 3: Rep row 2. Fasten off.

Sew buttons opposite buttonholes. Weave in ends. Block.

skill level ◆ beginner

skill level ◆ easy

Shoreline Cowl

◆ ⬦⬦⬦⬦⬦⬦⬦⬦⬦⬦⬦⬦⬦⬦⬦⬦ ◆ ⬦⬦⬦⬦⬦⬦⬦⬦⬦⬦⬦⬦⬦⬦⬦⬦ ◆

With a soft, textured shell stitch and
a sweet scalloped edge, this cowl
will keep you cozy in style.

◆ ◆ ◆

finished measurements

- 12½" deep x 30" circumference (32cm x 76cm)

materials and tools

- Bernat Super Value Yarn (100% acrylic; 7oz/197g = approx 426 yds/389m): 2 skeins, color lavender #53307—approx 852yd/778m of worsted weight yarn (4)

- Crochet hook: 11.50mm (size P-15 U.S.) or size to obtain gauge

- Yarn needle

gauge

- 8 dc and 4 rows = 4"/10cm with yarn held double

Always take time to check your gauge.

stitches used

- chain (ch)
- slip stitch (sl st)
- double crochet (dc)
- single crochet (sc)

Shoreline Cowl

instructions

With yarn held double, ch 60, join with a sl st in first ch to form a ring.

Rnd 1: Working in back loops only, ch 1, *sk 2 ch, 5 dc in next ch, sk 2 ch, sc in next ch; rep from * around, join with sl st in top of beg ch-1.

Rnd 2: Working in both loops, here and throughout, ch 3 (counts as first dc here and throughout), work 2 dc in same st as beg ch-3, *sk 2 sts, sc, sk 2 sts, work 5 dc in next st; rep from * around, end with 2 dc in same st as beg ch-3, join with sl-st in top of beg ch-3.

Rnd 3: Ch 1, *sk 2 sts, 5 dc in next st, sk 2 sts, sc in next st; rep from * around, join with sl st in beg ch-1.

Rnds 4–15: Rep rnds 2 and 3.

Fasten off.

Finishing

Using yarn needle, weave in ends.

Triangle Fringe Scarf

◆ ⬖⬗⬖⬗⬖⬗⬖⬗⬖⬗⬖⬗ ◆ ⬖⬗⬖⬗⬖⬗⬖⬗⬖⬗⬖⬗ ◆

With a larger hook and lighter yarn, create an intricate lace look from a simple pattern: Increases at the beginning and end of each row form simple triangles in this scarf.

◆ ◆ ◆

finished measurements

- Approx 55" wide x 28" deep (excluding fringe) (140cm x 71cm)

materials and tools

- Caron Spa (75% microdenier acrylic, 25% rayon from bamboo; 3oz/85g = 251yd/230m): 3 skeins, color stormy blue #0010—approx 753yd/690cm of DK weight yarn (3)

- Crochet hook: 11.50mm (size P-15 U.S.) or size to obtain gauge

- Yarn needle

- Scissors

- 9½"/24cm cardboard square

gauge

- 7 dc and 4 rows = 4"/10cm

Always take time to check your gauge.

stitches used

- chain (ch)

- double crochet (dc)

Triangle Fringe Scarf

instructions

When making slip knot, leave tail 9½"/24cm long to blend with fringe.

Ch 5.

Row 1: Dc in 5th ch from hook, [ch 1, dc] 3 times in same ch as first dc.

Row 2: Ch 4 (counts as first dc, ch-1 here and throughout), turn, dc in same st as beg ch-4, ch 1, *dc in next dc, ch 1; rep from * across to last dc, (dc, ch 1, dc) in next dc—6 dc and 5 ch-1 sp.

Row 3: Ch 4, turn, dc in same st as beg ch, ch 1, *dc in next dc, ch 1; rep from * across to last dc, (dc, ch 1, dc) in last dc—8 dc and 7 ch-1 sp.

Rows 4–27: Rep row 3—56 dc and 55 ch-1 sp. Fasten off, leaving tail 9½"/24cm long (blend with fringe).

Finishing

Fringe

Wrap yarn around 9½"/24cm cardboard square 170 times. Insert scissors under loops at one end and cut. Taking 3 strands at a time, attach fringe to ends of wrap as follows: Insert hook in st. Fold strands in half and place on hook, pull through st to form a loop. Draw ends through loop and pull tight to secure. Attach fringe to bottom point of triangle and along both short sides in each sp at beg of rows.

Using yarn needle, weave in ends.

skill level ◈ easy

Geraldine Circle Scarf

◆ ⬦⬦⬦⬦⬦⬦⬦⬦⬦⬦⬦⬦⬦ ◆ ⬦⬦⬦⬦⬦⬦⬦⬦⬦⬦⬦⬦⬦ ◆

*Chunky but delicate, textured but soft, and made
up quickly in bulky yarn, this circle scarf
pairs well with anything.*

◆ ◆ ◆

finished measurements

 ◆ 10" wide x 60" circumference (25cm x 152cm)

materials and tools

 ◆ Bernat Roving (80% acrylic, 20% wool; 3½oz/100g = 120yd/109m): 3 skeins, color amber #911078—approx 360yd/327m of bulky weight yarn (**5**)

 ◆ Crochet hook: 15.75mm (size Q-19 U.S.) or size to obtain gauge

 ◆ Yarn needle

gauge

 ◆ 5 dc and 3½ rows = 4"/10cm

Always take time to check your gauge.

stitches used

 ◆ chain (ch)

 ◆ slip stitch (sl st)

 ◆ single crochet (sc)

 ◆ double crochet (dc)

Geraldine Circle Scarf

instructions

Ch 75, join with a sl st in first ch to form a ring.

Rnd 1: Ch 1, 2 dc in same st as beg ch, sk 2 ch, *work (sc, 2 dc) in next ch, sk 2 ch; rep from * around, join with sl st in beg ch-1.

Rnd 2: Ch 1, 2 dc in same st as beg ch, sk 2 dc, *work (sc, 2 dc) in next sc, sk 2 dc; rep from * around, join with sl st in beg ch-1.

Rnds 3–10: Rep rnd 2.

Rnd 11: Ch 1, sc in each st around, join with sl st in beg ch-1.

Fasten off.

Finishing

Next rnd: Join yarn beg ch, ch 1, *work 2 sc in skipped ch-2, work 1 sc in next st; rep from * around, join with sl st in beg ch-1.

Fasten off. Using yarn needle, weave in ends.

Striped Tank

◆ ◇◇◇◇◇◇◇◇◇◇◇◇◇◇◇◇ ◆ ◇◇◇◇◇◇◇◇◇◇◇◇◇◇◇◇ ◆

*Light and airy enough for summer, yet roomy
enough for layering during the colder months.
Start this tank now and you'll be wearing it
by the end of the weekend.*

◆ ◆ ◆

finished measurements

- Bust: 34 (38, 42, 46, 50)" [86 (96, 107, 117, 127)cm]
- Length: 26 (26, 28, 28, 28)" [66 (66, 71, 71, 71)cm]

materials and tools

- Lion Brand Cotton-Ease (50% cotton, 50% acrylic; 3.5oz/100g = 207yd/188m): (A), 1 (1, 1, 2, 2) skeins, color terracotta #134; (B), 1 (1, 1, 2, 2) skeins, color taupe #122; (C), 1 (1, 1, 2, 2) skeins, color stone #149—approx 621 (621, 621, 1242, 1242, 1242)yd/564 (564, 564, 1128, 1128, 1128)m of worsted weight yarn (4)
- Crochet hook: 6.50mm (size K-10.5 U.S.) or size to obtain gauge
- Yarn needle

gauge

- 10 hdc and 6 rows = 4"/10cm

Always take time to check your gauge.

stitches used

- chain (ch)
- slip stitch (sl st)
- half double crochet (hdc)

Note: Tank is worked from the bottom up.

Striped Tank

instructions

Front and Back (make 2)

With A, ch 44 (50, 54, 60, 64).

Row 1: Hdc in third ch from hook and in each ch across—42 (48, 52, 58, 62) hdc.

Row 2: Ch 2 (counts as first hdc here and throughout), turn. Work hdc in each st across.

Row 3: Rep row 2. Change to B.

Rows 4–6: Rep row 2. Change to C.

Rows 7–9: Rep row 2. Change to B.

Rows 10–15: Rep row 2. Change to A.

Rows 16–19: Rep row 2. Change to B.

Rows 20–25: Rep row 2. Change to C.

Rows 26–27 (27, 28, 28, 28): Rep row 2.

Row 28 (28, 29, 29, 29): Turn, sl st in first 3 sts. Ch 2 (counts as hdc), hdc in each st across to last 2 sts. Turn, leaving these sts unworked—38 (44, 48, 54, 58) hdc.

Row 29 (29, 30, 30, 30): Rep last row—34 (40, 44, 50, 54) hdc.

Rows 30–31 (30–31, 31–32, 31–32, 31–32): Turn, sl st in first 3 (3, 4, 4, 5) sts. Ch 2 (counts as hdc), hdc in each st across to last 2 (2, 3, 3, 4) sts. Turn, leaving these sts unworked—26 (32, 32, 38, 38) hdc.

Row 32 (32, 33, 33, 33): Ch 2, turn. Work hdc in each st across.

Row 33 (33, 34, 34, 34): Rep last row. Do not fasten off.

Straps

Row 1: Ch 2, turn. Work hdc in next 4 sts.

Rep row 1 for 6 (6, 8, 8, 8) more rows. Fasten off.

Join yarn at opposite side and work in the same manner. Fasten off.

Finishing

Sew side seams and ends of straps. Using yarn needle, weave in ends. Block.

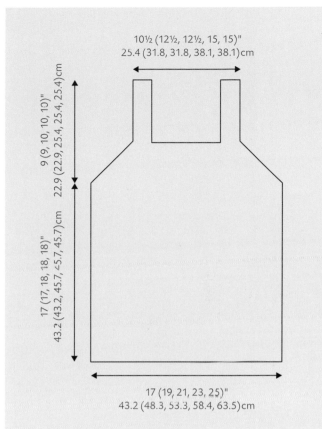

10½ (12½, 12½, 15, 15)"
25.4 (31.8, 31.8, 38.1, 38.1)cm

9 (9, 10, 10, 10)"
22.9 (22.9, 25.4, 25.4, 25.4)cm

17 (17, 18, 18, 18)"
43.2 (43.2, 45.7, 45.7, 45.7)cm

17 (19, 21, 23, 25)"
43.2 (48.3, 53.3, 58.4, 63.5)cm

skill level ◆ beginner

Striped Cotton Tote

◆ ⬦⬦⬦⬦⬦⬦⬦⬦⬦⬦⬦⬦ ◆ ⬦⬦⬦⬦⬦⬦⬦⬦⬦⬦⬦⬦ ◆

*Made up in a solid color or with a simple stripe,
this tote stitches up easily and with plenty of
room for your outing necessities.*

◆ ◆ ◆

finished measurements

- 16" tall (excluding strap) x 13" across (at top) (41cm x 33cm)

materials and tools

- Lily Sugar'n Cream Super Size (100% cotton; 4oz/113g = 200yd/184m): (A), 2 skeins, color indigo #01114; (B), 2 skeins, color wine #00015—approx 800yd/736m of worsted weight yarn (4)
- Crochet hook: 5.50mm (size I-9 U.S.) or size to obtain gauge
- Yarn needle

gauge

- 11 dc and 7 rows = 4"/10cm

Always take time to check your gauge.

stitches used

- chain (ch)
- slip stitch (sl st)
- double crochet (dc)
- single crochet (sc)
- double crochet two stitches together (dc2tog)

Striped Cotton Tote

instructions

With A, ch 3, join with a sl st in first ch to form a ring.

Rnd 1: Ch 2 (counts as first dc here and throughout), work 17 dc into ring, join with sl st in top of beg ch-2—18 sts.

Rnd 2: Ch 2, work 1 dc in same st as beg ch, work 2 dc in each st of prev rnd, join with sl st in top of beg ch-2—36 sts.

Rnd 3: Ch 2, dc, work 2 dc in next st, *dc in next 2 sts, 2 dc in next st; rep from * around, join with sl st in top of beg ch-2—48 sts.

Rnd 4: Ch 2, dc in next 2 sts, work 2 dc in next st, *dc in next 3 sts, 2 dc in next st; rep from * around, join with sl st in top of beg ch-2—60 sts.

Rnd 5: Ch 2, dc in next 3 sts, work 2 dc in next st, *dc in next 4 sts, 2 dc in next st; rep from * around, join with sl st in top of beg ch-2—72 sts.

Rnd 6: Ch 2, dc in next 4 sts, work 2 dc in next st, *dc in next 5 sts, 2 dc in next st; rep from * around, join with sl st in top of beg ch-2—84 sts.

Rnd 7: Ch 2, dc in next 5 sts, work 2 dc in next st, *dc in next 6 sts, 2 dc in next st; rep from * around, join with sl st in top of beg ch-2—96 sts.

Rnd 8: Ch 2, dc in next 6 sts, work 2 dc in next st, *dc in next 7 sts, 2 dc in next st; rep from * around, join with sl st in top of beg ch-2—108 sts. Change to B.

Rnd 9: Ch 2, dc in next 7 sts, work 2 dc in next st, *dc in next 8 sts, 2 dc in next st; rep from * around, join with sl st in top of beg ch-2—120 sts.

Rnd 10: Ch 2, dc in next 8 sts, work 2 dc in next st, *dc in next 9 sts, 2 dc in next st; rep from * around, join with sl st in top of beg ch-2—132 sts.

Rnd 11: Ch 2, work dc in each st around, join with sl st to top of beg ch-2—132 sts.

Rnds 12–13: Rep rnd 11. Change to A.

Rnds 14–17: Rep rnd 11.

Rnd 18: Ch 2, dc in next 8 sts, dc2tog, *dc in next 9 sts, dc2tog; rep from * around, join with sl st in top of beg ch-2—120 sts. Change to B.

Rnds 19–20: Rep rnd 11.

Rnd 21: Ch 2, dc in next 7 sts, dc2tog, *dc in next 8 sts, dc2tog; rep from * around, join with sl st in top of beg ch-2—108 sts.

Rnds 22–23: Rep rnd 11. Change to A.

Rnd 24: Ch 2, dc in next 6 sts, dc2tog, *dc in next 7 sts, dc2tog; rep from * around, join with sl st in top of beg ch-2—96 sts.

Rnd 25: Rep rnd 11.

Rnd 26: Ch 2, dc in next 5 sts, dc2tog, *dc in next 6 sts, dc2tog; rep from * around, join with sl st in top of beg ch-2—84 sts.

Rnd 27: Ch 2, dc in next 4 sts, dc2tog, *dc in next 5 sts, dc2tog; rep from * around, join with sl st in top of beg ch-2—72 sts.

Rnd 28: Rep rnd 11. Do not fasten off, continue for strap.

Strap

Row 1: Ch 2 (counts as first dc), dc in next 9 sts, turn—10 sts.

Rows 2–28: Rep row 1.

Sl st end of strap to opposite side of bag.

Fasten off.

Finishing

Using yarn needle, weave in ends.

Legwarmers

◆ ◇◇◇◇◇◇◇◇◇◇◇◇◇◇◇◇◇ ◆ ◇◇◇◇◇◇◇◇◇◇◇◇◇◇◇◇◇ ◆

Elegant and warm, the bamboo-blend yarn works
perfectly whether you want your legwarmers
pulled high or slouchy over flats.

◆ ◆ ◆

skill level ◆ beginner

finished measurements

- 17½" tall x 10" circumference
  (44cm x 25cm)

materials and tools

- Caron Spa (75% microdenier acrylic, 25% rayon from bamboo; 3oz/85g = 251yd/230m): 1 skein, color misty taupe #0008—approx 251yd/230m of DK weight yarn (3)

- Crochet hook: 6.50mm (size K-10.5 U.S.) or size to obtain gauge

- Elastic sewing thread

- Yarn needle

gauge

- 14 sc and 14 rows = 4"/10cm

Always take time to check your gauge.

stitches used

- chain (ch)

- slip stitch (sl st)

- single crochet (sc)

- double crochet (dc)

Legwarmers

instructions

Cut piece of elastic 7¼"/cm long. Knot ends together to form a circle, leaving approx ½"/1cm tail.

Rnd 1: Stitching around the elastic, ch 1 (counts as first sc here and throughout), work 37 sc around elastic circle. Join with sl st in beg ch-1—38 sc.

Rnd 2: Cut another piece of elastic as above and knot. Holding circle of elastic on top of sts of prev rnd, ch 1, sc in each st around. Join with sl st in beg ch-1.

Rnd 3: Rep rnd 2.

Rnd 4: Ch 1, sc in each st around. Join with sl st in beg ch-1.

Rnd 5: Ch 2 (counts as first dc here and throughout), sc in next st, *dc in next st, sc in next st; rep from * around, join with sl st in top of beg ch-2.

Rnd 6: Ch 1, work dc in next sc, *work sc in next dc, dc in next sc; rep from * around, join with sl st in beg ch-1.

Rnd 7: Ch 2, work sc in next dc, *work dc in next sc, sc in next dc; rep from * around, join with sl st in top of beg ch-2.

Rnds 8–50: Rep rnds 6–7.

Rnds 51–52: Ch 1, sc in each st around. Join with sl st in beg ch-1.

Fasten off.

Finishing

Using yarn needle, weave in ends.

Laptop Sleeve

◆ ⬧⬧⬧⬧⬧⬧⬧⬧⬧⬧⬧⬧⬧⬧ ◆ ⬧⬧⬧⬧⬧⬧⬧⬧⬧⬧⬧⬧⬧ ◆

This strapping bag will keep your laptop from getting bumped and scratched—there's nothing like a soft cover for your hardware.

◆ ◆ ◆

skill level ◆ beginner

finished measurements

* 10" tall x 14½" wide (25cm x 37cm)

materials and tools

* Lion Brand Cotton-Ease (50% cotton, 50% acrylic; 3.5oz/100g = 207yd/188m): 2 skeins, color golden glow #187—approx 414yd/376m of worsted weight yarn (4)

* Crochet hook: 5.50mm (size I-9 U.S.) or size to obtain gauge

* 4 – 1"/2.5cm D-rings

* 1yd/1m wide brown cotton belting, 1"/2.5cm wide

* 1 bottle of fray retardant

* Sewing needle and thread

* Yarn needle

gauge

* 11 sc and 12 rows = 4"/10cm

Always take time to check your gauge.

stitches used

* chain (ch)

* slip stitch (sl st)

* single crochet (sc)

Note: To adjust size to fit your laptop, measure its width and multiply by 2.75. Add 1 for turning chain and chain this amount. Work instructed until piece is twice as long as laptop, plus 6"/15cm for flap. Fasten off and finish as directed.

Laptop Sleeve

instructions

Ch 41.

Row 1: Sc in 2nd ch from hook, sc in each ch across—40 sc.

Row 2: Ch 1, sc in each across—40 sc.

Rows 3–79: Rep row 2.

Fasten off.

Finishing

Using yarn needle, weave in ends.

Lay piece flat with RS facing. Fold short end up 10"/25cm, leaving rem 6"/15cm for flap. Sew sides, turn to RS.

Upper Straps

Cut 2 pieces of belting, each 5"/13cm long. Loop one end of belting through 2 D-rings, with flat side of rings in fold. Pull strap through and fold over approx 1"/2.5cm. Pin and sew strap tog near raw edge to enclose rings. Fold other end of strap under ½"/1cm, pin and sew as before. Rep for second strap. Apply fray retardant to raw edges of each strap.

Measure 3"/8cm in from one side of flap and 2"/5cm up from bottom of flap and pin strap (with D-rings hanging to bottom). Sew strap in place. Rep for second strap.

Lower Straps

Cut 2 pieces of belting 7½"/19cm long. Fold one end of belting under ½"/1cm, pin and sew near raw edge. Fold other end of strap under ½"/1cm with raw edge turned toward opposite side (so raw edge will not show when bag is fastened), pin and sew near raw edge. Rep for second strap. Apply fray retardant to raw edges.

Measure 3"/8cm in from one side of bag and 1"/2.5cm up from bottom of bag (making sure to align with strap on flap) and pin. Sew strap in place. Rep for second strap.

Headwrap

◆ ✕✕✕✕✕✕✕✕✕✕✕✕✕ ◆ ✕✕✕✕✕✕✕✕✕✕✕✕✕ ◆

This headwrap combines the practicality of earwarmers with a retro look inspired by the glamorous turbans from the '20s and '30s.

◆ ◆ ◆

finished measurements

◆ 5½" wide x 22" circumference (14cm x 56cm)

materials and tools

◆ Patons Classic Wool (100% wool; 3.5oz/ 100g = 223yd/205m): 1 skein, color cognac heather #77532—approx 223yd/205m of worsted weight yarn (4)

◆ Crochet hook: 6.50mm (size K-10.5 U.S.) or size to obtain gauge

◆ Yarn needle

gauge

◆ 10 dc and 6 rows = 4"/10cm

Always take time to check your gauge.

stitches used

◆ chain (ch)

◆ slip stitch (sl st)

◆ double crochet (dc)

◆ single crochet (sc)

Headwrap

instructions

Ch 54, join with a sl st in first ch to form a ring.

Rnd 1: Ch 2 (counts as first dc here and throughout), sc in next st, *dc in next st, sc in next st; rep from * around, join with sl st in top of beg ch-2—54 sts.

Rnd 2: Ch 1 (counts as first sc here and throughout), work dc in next sc, *work sc in next dc, dc in next sc; rep from * around, join with sl st in beg ch-1.

Rnd 3: Ch 2, work sc in next dc, *work dc in next sc, sc in next dc; rep from * around, join with sl st in top of beg ch-2.

Rnds 4–11: Rep rnds 2 and 3.

Rnd 12: Rep rnd 2.

Rnd 13: Ch 1, work sc in each st around, join with sl st to beg ch-1.

Fasten off.

Finishing

Join yarn to bottom of piece. Ch 1, work sc evenly around. Join with sl st to beg ch-1.

Fasten off. Using yarn needle, weave in ends.

Center Wrap

Ch 8.

Row 1: Dc in 3rd ch from hook, *sc, dc; rep from * across to last st, sc in last st—7 sts.

Row 2: Ch 2 (counts as first dc), *sc, dc; rep from * across—7 sts.

Row 3: Ch 1, sc in first st, *dc in next sc, sc in next dc; rep from * across.

Rows 4–7: Rep rows 2 and 3.

Row 8: Rep row 2.

Without finishing off, wrap piece around one side of headwrap to gather. Sl st first and last rows tog to secure.

Fasten off.

Finishing

Using yarn needle, weave in ends.

skill level ◆ beginner

Button Clutch

◆ ✕✕✕✕✕✕✕✕✕✕✕✕✕✕ ◆ ✕✕✕✕✕✕✕✕✕✕✕✕✕✕ ◆

Carry the essentials while the rest of your outfit makes the statement. Day or night, this little clutch just may be the perfect accessory.

◆ ◆ ◆

finished measurements

◦ 10" wide x 6" tall (25cm x 15cm)

materials and tools

◦ Lion Brand Baby's First (55% acrylic, 45% cotton; 3.5oz/100g = 120yd/110m): 1 skein, color pixie dust #099—approx 120yd/110m of bulky weight yarn **(5)**

◦ Crochet hook: 6.00mm (size J-10 U.S.) and 5.50mm (size I-9 U.S) or sizes to obtain gauge

◦ Yarn needle

◦ 1 – 1"/2.5cm button

gauge

◦ 10 sc and 10 rows = 4"/10cm using larger hook

Always take time to check your gauge.

stitches used

◦ chain (ch)

◦ slip stitch (sl st)

◦ single crochet (sc)

◦ double crochet (dc)

Button Clutch

instructions

With larger hook, ch 28.

Row 1: In 4th ch from hook, work 2 sc, *sk next ch, work 2 sc in next ch; rep from * across—26 sc.

Row 2: Ch 2, turn. *Sk next st, work 2 sc in next st; rep from * across.

Rows 3–26: Rep row 2. Do not fasten off.

Finishing

Lay piece flat with RS facing. Fold piece in half from bottom to top and seam up each side with sl st. Fasten off. Turn to RS.

With smaller hook and RS facing, join yarn in any stitch at top opening. Work 4 rnds of sc evenly around top edge, fasten off.

Button Loop

Join yarn at center top edge of bag. Ch 8, sl st back in first ch to form loop. Fasten off. Using yarn needle, weave in ends. Sew button opposite button loop.

Fingerless Mitts

◆ ⋈⋈⋈⋈⋈⋈⋈⋈⋈⋈⋈⋈⋈ ◆ ⋈⋈⋈⋈⋈⋈⋈⋈⋈⋈⋈⋈⋈ ◆

*Mitts are a great option when you need
to keep your fingers free for typing, using
your phone, or stitching on the go.*

◆ ◆ ◆

skill level ◆ easy

finished measurements

- 5" tall x 7" circumference (13cm x 18cm)

materials and tools

- Bernat Alpaca Natural Blends (70% acrylic, 30% alpaca; 3.5oz/100g = 120yd/110m): 1 skein, color sky #93143—approx 120yd/110m of bulky weight yarn (5)

- Crochet hook: 6.50mm (size K-10.5 U.S.) or size to obtain gauge

- Yarn needle

gauge

- 10 dc and 5 rows = 4"/10cm

Always take time to check your gauge.

stitches used

- chain (ch)

- slip stitch (sl st)

- double crochet (dc)

- single crochet (sc)

Fingerless Mitts

instructions

Ch 18, join with a sl st in first ch to form a ring.

Rnd 1: Ch 1 (counts as first sc here and throughout), work 2 dc in same st as beg ch, *sk next 2 sts, work (sc, 2 dc) in next st; rep from * around, sk last 2 sts, join with sl st in beg ch-1.

Rnds 2–3: Rep rnd 1.

Rnd 4: Ch 1, work 2 dc in same st as beg ch, sk next 2 sts, work (sc, 2 dc) in next st, ch 3, sk next 5 sts (thumb opening), *work (sc, 2 dc) in next st, sk 2 sts; rep from * around, join with sl st in beg ch-1.

Rnd 5: Ch 1, work 2 dc in same st as beg ch, sk next 2 sts, work (sc, 2 dc) in next st, sk next 2 sts, work (sc, 2 dc) in first ch, sk next 2 ch, *work (sc, 2 dc) in next st, sk 2 sts; rep from * around, join with sl st in beg ch-1.

Rnd 6: Rep rnd 1.

Rnd 7: Ch 1, sc in each st around, join with sl st to beg ch-1—18 sc.

Rnds 8–10: Rep rnd 7.

Fasten off.

Finishing

Join hook to opposite end of mitt and work 2 rnds of sc (top of mitt).

Finish off. Using yarn needle, weave in ends.

Small Bow Pin

Perfect to make and give, this sweet little bow is quick to stitch. Work one up in every color.

skill level ◆ easy

finished measurements:

- 2" tall x 3¼" wide (assembled) (5cm x 8cm)

materials and tools

- Caron Simply Soft (100% acrylic; 6oz/170g = 315yd/288m): 1 skein, color tomato #93531—approx 315yd/288m of worsted weight yarn (4)

- Crochet hook: 3.75mm (size F-5 U.S.) or size to obtain gauge

- Yarn needle

- Silvertone metal bobby pin with pad

- Hot glue gun

gauge

- 16 sc and 16 rows = 4"/10cm

Always take time to check your gauge.

stitches used

- chain (ch)
- slip stitch (sl st)
- single crochet (sc)

Small Bow Pin

instructions

Ch 14.

Row 1: Ch 1, sc in 2nd ch from hook and each ch across, turn—13 sc.

Row 2: Work sc in back loop of each st, turn.

Rows 3–8: Rep row 2.

Fasten off.

Finishing

Cut strand of yarn approx 48"/122cm long. Leaving a tail for tying, wrap around center of rectangle approx 15 times to cinch into bow shape. Tie ends of strand together at back of bow with a double knot.

Using yarn needle, weave in ends.

Using hot glue gun, attach bow to pad of bobby pin. Let dry.

Bamboo Handle Bag

◆ ◇◇◇◇◇◇◇◇◇◇◇◇◇◇◇ ◆ ◇◇◇◇◇◇◇◇◇◇◇◇◇◇◇ ◆

Tote your crochet projects, market finds, and more. A traditional Catherine wheel stitch showcases this wool-blend yarn.

skill level ◈ intermediate

finished measurements

- 14½" tall (excluding handles) x 17½" wide (at base) (36 x 44cm)

materials and tools

- Bernat Roving (80% acrylic, 20% wool; 3.5oz/100g = 120yd/109m): 3 skeins, color orchid #00332— approx 360yd/327m of bulky weight yarn (5)

- Crochet hook: 9.00mm (size N-13 U.S.) or size to obtain gauge

- 8½ x 5½" (22 x 14cm) oval bamboo purse handles

- Yarn needle

gauge

- 7 dc and 4 rows = 4"/10cm

Always take time to check your gauge.

Bamboo Handle Bag

instructions

Bag Side (make 2)

Work 46 sc around one bamboo handle—46 sc.

Row 1: Ch 1, work sc in first 2 sts, *sk next 3 sts, work 7 dc in next st, sk next 3 sts, sc in next 3 sts; rep from * across to last 4 sts, sk next 3 sts, work 4 dc in last st. Turn.

Row 2: Ch 1, work sc in same st, sc in next st, *ch 3, work 7-dc cl, ch 3, sc in next 3 sts (careful not to work in side of last st of cluster); rep from * across to last 4 sts, ch 3, work 4-dc cl in last 4 sts. Turn.

Row 3: Ch 3 (counts as first dc here and throughout), work 3 dc in same st, *sk next ch-3 sp, sc in next 3 sc, sk next 2 ch, work 7 dc in next ch; rep from * across to last ch-3 sp, sk last ch-3 sp, sc in last 2 sc. Turn.

stitches used

- chain (ch)
- slip stitch (sl st)
- double crochet (dc)
- single crochet (sc)
- double crochet cluster (dc cl)

special stitches

- **7-dc cluster (7-dc cl):** [Yo, insert hook in next st, yo and draw up a loop, yo, draw through 2 loops on hook] 7 times, yo and draw through all 8 loops on hook.

- **4-dc cluster (4-dc cl):** [Yo, insert hook in next st, yo and draw up a loop, yo, draw through 2 loops on hook] 4 times, yo and draw through all 5 loops on hook.

- **3-dc cluster (3-dc cl):** [Yo, insert hook in next st, yo and draw up a loop, yo, draw through 2 loops on hook] 3 times, yo and draw through all 4 loops on hook.

Row 4: Ch 3, in next st work 3-dc cl, *ch 3, sc in next 3 sts, ch 3, work 7-dc cl; rep from * across to last 2 sts, ch 3, sc in last 2 sts. Turn.

Row 5: Ch 1, sc in same st, sc in next st, *sk next 2 ch, work 7 dc in next ch, sk next ch-3 sp, sc in next 3 sc; rep from * across to last ch-3 sp, sk last ch-3 sp, work 4 dc in last st. Turn.

Rows 6–17: Rep rows 2–5.

Row 18: Rep row 2.

Row 19: Ch 1, sc in same st, *(careful not to work in side of clusters) work 3 sc in next 3 ch, sc in next 3 sts, 3 sc in next 3 ch; rep from * across to last ch-3 sp, work 3 sc in next 3 ch, sc in last 2 sts.

Row 20: Ch 1, sc in each st across.

Fasten off.

Finishing

With WS facing and starting 4"/10cm down from handle, join sides using sl st, working around bottom and stopping 4"/10cm from handle on opposite side.

Fasten off. Using yarn needle, weave in ends. Turn to RS.

Rainbow Shell Throw

◆ ◇◇◇◇◇◇◇◇◇◇◇◇◇◇◇◇ ◆ ◇◇◇◇◇◇◇◇◇◇◇◇◇◇◇◇ ◆

The rainbow after the storm—this cascade of color set against a stormy grey backdrop will add a splash of happiness anywhere it lies.

◆ ◆ ◆

finished measurements

- 58" long x 50" wide (147cm x 127cm)

materials and tools

- Lion Brand Jiffy Yarn (100% acrylic; 3oz/85g = 135yd/123m): (A), 3 skeins, color dark grey heather #159; (B), 1 skein, color shocking pink #196; (C), 2 skeins, color chili #115; (D), 1 skein, color rust #135; (E), 2 skeins, color citron #129; (F) 1 skein, color apple green #132; (G), 2 skeins, color denim #107; (H), 1 skein, color grape #138—approx 1755yd/1599m of worsted weight yarn (4)

- Crochet hook: 11.50mm (size P-15 U.S.) or size to obtain gauge

- Yarn needle

gauge

- 7 dc and 4 rows = 4"/10cm

Always take time to check your gauge.

stitches used

- chain (ch)

- double crochet (dc)

- shell

special stitches

- Shell: Work 5 dc in same st or ch-sp.

Rainbow Shell Throw

instructions

With A, ch 92.

Row 1: Sc in 2nd ch from hook, *sk 2 ch, 5 dc in next ch (shell made), sk 2 ch, 1 sc in next ch; rep from * across.

Row 2: Ch 3 (counts as first dc here and throughout), turn. Work 2 dc in first sc, *sc in center dc of next shell, 5 dc in next sc; rep from * across, end with 3 dc in last sc—14 full shells, 2 half shells.

Row 3: Ch 1 (counts as first sc here and throughout), turn. Work 1 sc in first dc, *5 dc in next sc, 1 sc in center dc of next shell; rep from * across, end with 1 sc in top of turning ch—15 shells.

*Rep rows 2 and 3, changing colors as follows:

1 row B

2 rows C

1 row D

2 rows E

1 row F

2 rows G

1 row H

3 rows A

Rep from * a total of 5 times.

Fasten off.

Finishing

Using yarn needle, weave in ends.

Sweetheart Garland

◆ ⟨×××××××××××××××⟩ ◆ ⟨×××××××××××××××⟩ ◆

Dress your nest with these sweet little hearts.
Try them in a doorway, draped over a bookshelf,
or hanging on your headboard.

◆ ◆ ◆

finished measurements

- Large heart: 2½" tall x 3" wide (6cm x 8cm)
- Small heart: 2" tall x 2½" wide (5cm x 6cm)

materials and tools

- Caron Simply Soft (100% acrylic; 6oz/170g = 315yd/288m): (A), 1 skein, color autumn red #9730; (B), 1 skein, color soft pink #9719; (C), 1 skein, color white #9701—approx 945yd/864m of worsted weight yarn (4)
- Crochet hook: 3.75mm (size F-5 U.S.) or size to obtain gauge
- Yarn needle

gauge

- 16 dc and 8 rows = 4"/10cm

Always take time to check your gauge.

stitches used

- chain (ch)
- slip stitch (sl st)
- single crochet (sc)
- double crochet (dc)

Sweetheart Garland

instructions

Large Heart (make 5)

With A, ch 4, join with a sl st in first ch to form a ring.

Rnd 1: Ch 3, work 2 dc in ring, ch 2, work (3 dc, ch 2) in ring 3 more times. Join with sl st in top of beg ch-3.

Rnd 2: Ch 1, sc in next 2 dc, sc in next ch-2 sp, sk next dc, work 8 dc in next dc, sk next dc, work sl st down into beg center ring to cinch heart, ch 1, sk next dc, work 8 dc in next dc, sk next dc, work sc in next ch-2 sp, sc in next 3 dc, work sc in next ch-2 sp, join with sl st in beg ch-1.

Rnd 3: Ch 1, sc in next 6 st, work 2 dc in each of next 4 dc, sl st in next st, sk center st, sl st in next st, work 2 dc in each of next 4 dc, work sc in remaining st around to last st, dc in last st, join with sl st in beg ch-1. Fasten off.

Small Heart (make 6)

With B, ch 4, join with a sl st in first ch to form a ring.

Rnd 1: Ch 3, work 2 dc in ring, ch 2, work (3 dc, ch 2) in ring 3 more times. Join with sl st in top of beg ch-3.

Rnd 2: Ch 1, sc in next 2 dc, sc in next ch-2 sp, sk next dc, work 8 dc in next dc, sk next dc, work sl st down into beg center ring to cinch heart, ch 1, sk next dc, work 8 dc in next dc, sk next dc, work sc in next ch-2 sp, sc in next 3 dc, work sc in next ch-2 sp, join with sl st in beg ch-1. Fasten off.

Finishing

With C, ch 40, *in small heart, sc in 4th dc to the right of top center, ch 6, sc in 4th dc to the left of top center, ch 16; in large heart, sc in 4th dc to the right of top center, ch 6, sc in 4th dc to the left of top center, ch 16; rep from * across until all hearts are joined. Ch 40, fasten off.

Using yarn needle, weave in ends.

Lovely Little Lampshade

◆ ✕✕✕✕✕✕✕✕✕✕✕✕✕ ◆ ✕✕✕✕✕✕✕✕✕✕✕✕✕ ◆

*Revamp your lamp and cast a new light on
your everyday décor.*

◆ ◆ ◆

finished measurements

- 6¼" high x 7" top diameter x 8½" bottom diameter (16cm x 18cm x 22cm)

materials and tools

- Lion Brand Cotton-Ease (50% cotton, 50% acrylic; 3.5oz/100g = 207yd/188m): (A), 2 skeins, color golden glow #187; (B), 2 skeins, color terracotta #134—approx 828yd/376m of worsted weight yarn (4)
- Crochet hook: 11.50mm (size P-15 U.S.) or size needed to obtain gauge
- 6¼" high x 6¼" top diameter x 8" bottom diameter (16cm x 16cm x 20cm) lampshade
- Fabric glue (optional)
- Yarn needle

gauge

- 6 sc and 13 rows = 4"/10cm with yarn held double, after stretching over lampshade

Always take time to check your gauge.

stitches used
- chain (ch)
- slip stitch (sl st)
- single crochet (sc)

Lovely Little Lampshade

instructions

With 2 strands of A, ch 28, join with sl st in first ch to form a ring.

Rnd 1: Ch 1 (counts as first sc here and throughout), sc in each st around, join with sl st in beg ch-1—28 sc.

Rnds 2–3: Rep rnd 1.

Rnd 4: Ch 1, sc in next 12 sts, work 2 sc in next st, sc in next 13 sts, work 2 sc in next st, join with sl st to beg ch-1—30 sc. Change to B.

Rnds 5–6: Rep rnd 1. Change to A.

Rnd 7: Ch 1, sc in next 13 sts, work 2 sc in next st, sc in next 14 sts, work 2 sc in next st, join with sl st in beg ch-1—32 sc.

Rnds 8–9: Rep rnd 1. Change to B.

Rnd 10: Ch 1, sc in next 14 sts, work 2 sc in next st, sc in next 15 sts, work 2 sc in next st, join with sl st in beg ch-1—34 sc.

Rnds 11: Rep rnd 1. Change to A.

Rnds 12–13: Rep rnd 1.

Rnd 14: Ch 1, sc in next 15 sts, work 2 sc in next st, sc in next 16 sts, work 2 sc in next st, join with sl st to beg ch-1—36 sc. Change to B.

Rnds 15–16: Rep rnd 1. Change to A.

Rnds 17–21: Rep rnd 1.

Fasten off.

Finishing

Using yarn needle, weave in ends.

Pull finished cover over lampshade. Arrange to fit so rows are straight. If desired, secure with fabric glue and allow to dry.

skill level ◆ beginner

Granny Square Cushion

◆ ⬦⬦⬦⬦⬦⬦⬦⬦⬦⬦⬦⬦⬦⬦⬦⬦⬦ ◆ ⬦⬦⬦⬦⬦⬦⬦⬦⬦⬦⬦⬦⬦⬦⬦⬦⬦ ◆

*Insert some color into your world with this
cozy jewel-toned cushion cover, created from
a simple granny square pattern.*

◆ ◆ ◆

finished measurements

◦ 20" tall x 20" wide (51cm x 51cm)

materials and tools

◦ Lion Brand Wool-Ease Worsted Weight (80% acrylic, 20% wool; 3oz/85g = 197yd/180m): (A), 1 skein, color azalea #195; (B), 2 skeins, color cranberry #138; (C), 2 skeins, color eggplant #167; (D), 1 skeins, color dark rose heather #139—approx 1182yd/1080m of worsted weight yarn ❹

◦ Crochet hook: 5.00mm (size H-8 U.S.) or size to obtain gauge

◦ Yarn needle

◦ 20" x 20" (51cm x 51cm) pillow form

gauge

◦ 14 dc and 7 rows = 4"/10cm

Always take time to check your gauge.

stitches used

◦ chain (ch)

◦ slip stitch (sl st)

◦ single crochet (sc)

◦ double crochet (dc)

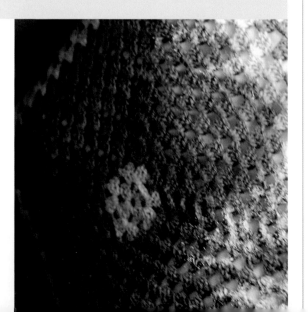

Granny Square Cushion

instructions

Front and Back (make 2)

With A, ch 4, join with a sl st in first ch to form a ring.

Rnd 1: Ch 3 (counts as dc, here and throughout), work 2 dc in ring, ch 2, work [3 dc, ch 2] in ring 3 more times. Join with sl st in top of beg ch-3.

Rnd 2: Sl st to ch-2 corner sp, ch 3, work (2 dc, ch 2, 3 dc) in same corner, work [ch-1, in next corner 3 dc, ch 2, 3 dc] 3 times. Join with sl st in top of beg ch-3. Fasten off.

Join B in any ch-2 corner sp.

Rnd 3: Ch 3, work (2 dc, ch 2, 3 dc) in same corner, *work (ch 1, 3 dc)** in each ch-1 sp on side of square, in corner ch-2 sp work (ch 1, 3 dc, ch 2, 3 dc); rep from * around, ending at **, ch 1 and join with sl st in top of beg ch-3.

Rnd 4: Sl st to ch-2 corner, rep rnd 3. Fasten off.

Rep rnds 3 and 4, changing colors every 2 rnds in the following sequence: C, D, C, B, C, B.

Finishing

Using yarn needle, weave in ends. With WS facing, sew front and back tog on 3 sides. Turn to RS, insert pillow form. Sew rem side.

basic stitches & techniques

To create beautiful items in crochet, you really only need to know a few basic stitches. Once you become comfortable with these basics and move on to more intricate pattern stitches, you'll be surprised to find that these stitches are largely just various combinations of the basics you've already learned! Below is an introduction for the beginner (or a refresher course for those who need it) to the basic stitches and techniques found in the patterns of this book.

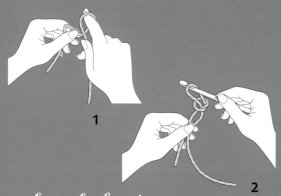

making the first loop

The first loop you make to insert onto your hook is created with a slip knot. To make a slip knot, hold the yarn between the thumb and middle finger of your left hand with the tail falling down toward the wrist. Wrap the yarn over the top and behind the index finger and under the middle finger. Wrap again over the index finger and pull a loop of yarn through the middle of the circle on your hand. While pulling this loop up with the right hand and holding the tail with your left hand, slip the circle off of your fingers. Tighten by pulling the tail. Loop may be made smaller to fit your hook by gently pulling the yarn feeding from the skein. This loop does not count as your first stitch.

chain stitch (ch)

The chain stitch (ch) is the starting point for most all crochet projects. It is often used to create the foundation for the first row or round of your project.

To make: Start with a slip knot and pull the loop snugly around the hook. Yarn over (yo) and pull the yarn through the loop on the hook—first chain made. Continue with the previous step until the desired number of stitches are made.

Tip: When creating your foundation row, do not make your chain stitches too tight or it will be difficult to insert your hook for the next row. This may also cause your work to curl at the sides or edges.

slip stitch (sl st)

The slip stitch (sl st) is the shortest stitch in crochet. It is often used to travel across to other stitches without adding height or to join stitches at the end of rounds. It is also helpful for seaming sides and pieces together.

To make: Insert hook into stitch. Yarn over (yo) and pull back through the stitch as well as through the loop on the hook.

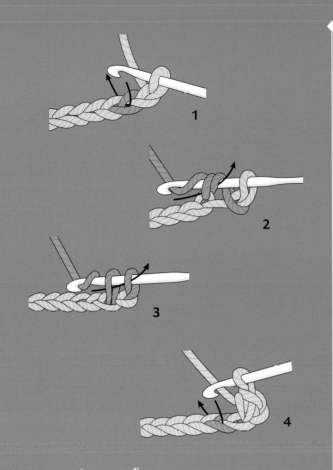

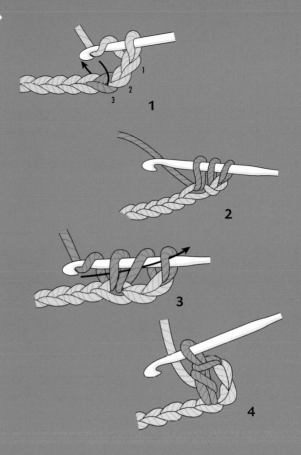

single crochet (sc)

The single crochet stitch (sc) adds just a bit of height. It makes a rather firm, solid fabric, and it's used for seaming in some instances.

To make: Insert hook into stitch. Yarn over (yo) and pull back through the stitch, yo and pull through two loops on the hook.

half double crochet (hdc)

The half double crochet stitch (hdc) allows your project to work up a bit faster than single crochet without being as loose and airy as double crochet.

To make: Yarn over (yo) and insert hook into stitch. Yo and pull the yarn back through the stitch, yo and pull through three loops on the hook.

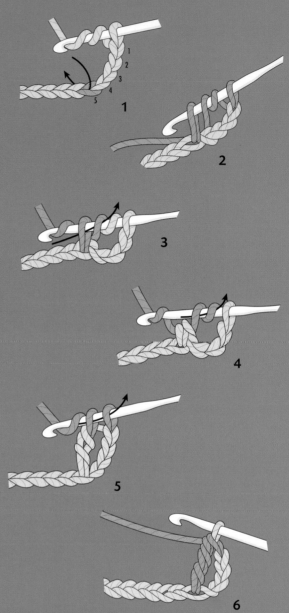

double crochet (dc)

The double crochet stitch (dc) gives height to your project and also forms a fabric that is lighter with a nice drape. It is one of the most commonly used stitches in crochet patterns.

To make: Yarn over (yo) and insert hook into stitch. Yo and pull the yarn back through the stitch, yo and pull through two loops, yo and pull through remaining two loops on the hook.

treble crochet (tr)

The treble crochet stitch (tr) is also referred to as the triple crochet. It is one of the tallest stitches used and creates an open and airy fabric.

To make: Yarn over (yo) and insert hook into stitch. Yo and pull the yarn back through the stitch, [yo and pull through 2 loops] twice, yo and pull through remaining two loops on the hook.

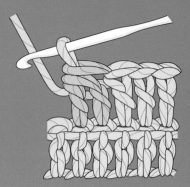

double crochet 2 together (dc2tog)

Also known as a double crochet decrease, this stitch allows you to shape your work by making it smaller in certain areas. It is worked over two stitches so that they become one.

To make: Yarn over (yo) and insert hook into stitch. Yo and pull the yarn back through the stitch, yo and pull through two loops. Yo and insert hook into next stitch. Yo and pull the yarn back through the stitch, yo and pull through two loops, yo and pull through remaining three loops on the hook.

other techniques

Here are a few techniques you'll need to know to create the projects in this book.

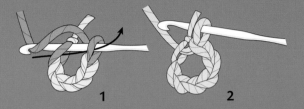

1   **2**

working in the round

When items are not worked side to side in rows, they are often worked in rounds. To work in the round you begin by stitching the desired number of chains and with a slip stitch, then join the last chain worked with the first chain to form a ring. This is the foundation to begin your project. From this point you will chain up and work the first round of stitches into the center of the ring. Some projects require you to join the last stitch of the round with a slip stitch to the first stitch of the round, while others require you to work in a continuous spiral.

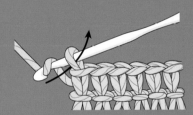

fastening off

Once you've completed a section of your project or the final row or round of your piece, you are ready to fasten off. This is done by simply cutting the yarn, being sure to leave a tail at least 4" (10cm) long, and pulling it through the last loop on the hook. Pull gently to secure the knot.

blocking

For items that are to be seamed or for items that require a set shape, you'll need to block your pieces. Blocking helps to shape your item and smooth the stitches for a more uniform look. Blocking is not required for certain types of scarves and cowls that can often be worn right off the hook, but it is important for clothing and other items that are seamed or for items that have a tendency to curl. Though curling can also be an outcome of too tight tension, which blocking can sometimes help.

To block pieces, fill a sink with lukewarm water (do not use hot water as it can cause changes in wool and other fibers). Dip your piece into the sink so that water fully absorbs into the yarn. Do not twist or agitate. Gently squeeze (careful not to twist) as much excess water from the piece as you can and pin it flat on a surface such as a cork board or ironing board that is covered by a thick towel, shaping it to your desired look and size. Leave the piece to dry. To be honest, blocking is something I rarely do unless I am creating pieces to be starched, so this step is entirely your choice and should depend upon how much confidence you have in the final shape of your piece once it is off the hook. Some swear by this step while others often skip it.

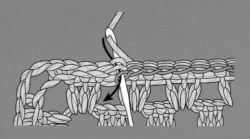

joining seams

There are many different methods for joining seams, depending on the type of item you are creating. Some items may require a more flexible seam while others may need a stronger, sturdier seam. For projects in this book, items are joined using the slip stitch method. To create this type of seam, place pieces with right sides facing each other and aligning the stitches to match on each side. To join with a slip stitch, insert the hook in the back loop of the stitch on the piece closest to you and into the front loop of the stitch of the piece farthest from you, and work slip stitches along the sides in this manner. If you prefer, you may also thread a yarn needle with your yarn and seam the pieces by using a basic whipstitch. Some prefer this method since it creates a less bulky seam.

weaving ends

Once you have finished stitching and constructing your item, you will notice a few loose threads hanging from your project. These are easily taken care of with your yarn needle. Thread the yarn through the eye of your needle and insert the needle into the neighboring stitches. Weave the yarn through the stitches to hide and encase the ends. It is best to weave the entire length of the tail since this well help prevent your work from coming apart or fraying down the road.

crochet abbreviations

ABBR	DESCRIPTION	ABBR	DESCRIPTION	ABBR	DESCRIPTION
[ ]	work instructions within brackets as many times as directed	dc2tog	double crochet 2 stitches together	p	picot
( )	work instructions within parenthesesas many times as directed	dec	decrease/decreases/decreasing	pat(s) or patt	patterns
* *	repeat instructions between asterisks as many times as directed or repeat from a given set of instructions	dtr	double treble	PM	place marker
*	repeat instructions following the single asterisk as directed	fl	front loop(s)	pop	popcorn
"	inches	foll	follow/follows/following	prev	previous
alt	alternate	FP	front post	rem	remain/remaining
approx	approximately	FPdc	front post double crochet	rep	repeat(s)
beg	beginning	FPsc	front post single crochet	rnd(s)	round(s)
bet	between	FPtr	front post treble crochet	RS	right side
BL	back loop(s)	fl	front loop(s)	sc	single crochet
bo	bobble	foll	follow/follows/following	sc2tog	single crochet 2 stitches together
BP	back post	FP	front post	sk	skip
BPdc	back post double crochet	FPdc	front post double crochet	sl st	slip stitch
BPsc	back post single crochet	FPsc	front post single crochet	sp(s)	space(s)
BPtr	back post treble crochet	FPtr	front post treble crochet	st(s)	stitch(es)
CA	color A	g	grams	tbl	through back loop
CB	color B	hdc	half double crochet	tch	turning chain
CC	contrasting color	inc	increase/increases/increasing	tog	together
ch	chain stitch	invdec	invisible decrease	tr	treble crochet
ch-	refers to chain or space previously made; e.g., ch-1 space	lp(s)	loop(s)	trtr	triple treble crochet
ch-sp	chain space	m	meters	WS	wrong side
CL	cluster	MC	main color	yd(s)	yard(s)
cm	centimeter(s)	mm	millimeter(s)	yo	yarn over
cont	continue	mr	make ring	yoh	yarn over hook
dc	double crochet	oz	ounce(s)		

yarn weight and crochet hook equivalents chart

Yarn Weight Symbol & Category Names	**1** Super Fine	**2** Fine	**3** Light	**4** Medium	**5** Bulky	**6** Super Bulky
Type of Yarns in Category	Fingering, Baby	Sport, Sock	DK, Light Worsted	Worsted, Afghan, Aran	Chunky, Craft, Rug	Bulky, Roving
Crochet Gauge* Ranges in Single Crochet to 4 inch	21-32 sts	16-20 sts	12-17 sts	11-14 sts	8-11 sts	5-9 sts
Recommended Hook in Metric Size Range	2.25-3.5 mm	3.5-4.5 mm	4.5-5.5 mm	5.5-6.5 mm	6.5-9 mm	9 mm and larger
Recommended Hook U.S. Size Range	B-1 to E-4	E-4 to 7	7 to I-9	I-9 to K-10½	K-10½ to M-13	M-13 and larger

Source: Craft Yarn Council of America's www.YarnStandards.com

regional crochet abbreviations

ABBR	U.S. TERM	ABBR	U.K./AUS TERM
sl st	slip st	sc	single crochet
sc	single crochet	dc	double crochet
hdc	half double crochet	htr	half treble crochet
dc	double crochet	tr	treble crochet
tr	treble crochet	dtr	double treble crochet
dtr	double treble crochet	trip tr or trtr	triple treble crochet
trtr	triple treble crochet	qtr	quadruple treble crochet
rev sc	reverse single crochet	rev dc	reverse double crochet
yo	yarn over	yoh	yarn over hook

about the author

*R*achael Oglesby lives in Columbia, South Carolina, by way of Natchez, Mississippi. She made the leap from her 9 to 5 career in library science to pursue her craft and has been designing and creating items for her business, softspoken, for the past five years. Her work has been sold through Modcloth, Etsy, and at many small boutiques both nationwide and globally. Find more of her work at **http://softspoken.us.**

acknowledgments

*F*irst, thanks to the staff at Lark who had enough confidence in me to allow me to write this book. Special thanks to Kathleen McCafferty for opening the door to this special venture and for being a supportive friend throughout the process. I also have to thank Amanda Carestio for doing so much work as my editor—she has helped me through each step of this process, listened to my concerns, and devoted so much time to bringing this all together. I am also grateful for the generosity of Plymouth Yarn, Caron, and Bernat and the yarn support they provided.

I also want to thank my photographer, Emily Ogden. A longtime friend, I am so ecstatic that Emily and I were able to work on this project together. There is no other person I would trust as much to realize my vision into a set of beautiful images. I am so lucky to have her on board with this project. I'm forever grateful for the hours and devotion she has given and for being so patient and encouraging, even through the stressful moments.

Thanks to my friend, Ann Holderfield. Over the course of our friendship she has given me the confidence to think of myself as an artist. I am grateful for our conversations and for her constant support and enthusiasm.

Loving thanks to Milton Hall—one of my biggest supporters and often my most honest critic. I can always trust him for his straightforward opinion and he has helped steer me away from many a design mishap. He has been there for my excitements and also encouraged me through my frustrations. Special thanks to Charlie Hall for just being himself. I am grateful for my years with these two boys.

Thanks to my family and all they've given me through the years. I'm lucky to have adoring grandparents who were there for me throughout my childhood. Thanks to my brother, Daniel, for all our memories growing up. And to my sweet nephew, Eli, who causes us all to see the world with fresh eyes.

And most importantly, thanks to my mom who taught me to crochet at an early age after many nights spent by her side watching her stitch up gifts for our family. Not only am I grateful for the craft she passed on to me, but also for her continued love and constant support through both the highest and lowest times of my life. Both of my parents, Keith and Tammy Oglesby, are the greatest parents one could ask for.

A special thanks to Hannah Bolvi, Valerie Ogden, Olivia Ogden, Johanna Schmidt, Kristen Eisentrager, and Corey Thomas for modeling my designs so well.

index